Chapter – 1

India's First Trick Based Study Material

SOME BASIC CONCEPTS OF CHEMISTRY

1 BASIC CONCEPT ON CHEMISTRY

1. WHAT IS CHEMISTRY?

"Chemistry is the branch of science that deals with the composition, properties and interaction of matter".

While going through this package, if you have a glance at your surroundings you would observe various substances that have different forms and appearances. Some substances are gases, some are liquids while the others are solids. Some of them are hard and shinning but others are soft and dull. You would also observe that different substances behave differently: Iron rusts but gold does not, copper conducts electricity but sulphur does not. The question now arises is how can these and a vast number of other observations be explained? Chemistry tries to answer to all these queries through experiments and formulation of an interpretation or hypothesis that explains the results. The hypothesis, in turn, can be used to make more predictions and to suggest more experiments until a consistent explanation or theory of known observation is finally arrived at.

It is important to keep in mind that scientific theories are not laws of nature. All they do is to represent the best explanations of experimental results that we can come up with at the present time. Some currently accepted theories will eventually be modified and others may be replaced altogether if new experiments uncover results that present theories can't explain.

2 MATTER

Anything which has mass and occupies space is known as **matter**. Water, gold, rocks, buildings, plants, animals and people are matter. Matter having specific use is termed as **material**. For example cement, glass, wood, paper etc. are matter but are also termed as material on account of their specific use. Solid, liquid and gaseous states represent the three different states of aggregation and provide a basis of the physical classification of matter. Gaseous state of matter at very high temperatures containing gaseous ions and free electrons is referred to as the **plasma state**.

Description of matter merely in terms of aggregation does not suffice and it becomes necessary to make use of another property to obtain a more useful classification of matter. One such useful way studied by you at the secondary stage, is to classify matter into the following categories: pure substances (elements, compounds) and mixtures. An element consists of only one kind of atoms. Molecules are identifiable units of matter consisting of two atoms of the same element or of different elements combined in a definite ratio. Mono, di or polyatomic molecules or extended structures with the same kind of atoms constitute elements while in a compound two or more than two different types of atoms are present. Thus a sample of pure hydrogen or oxygen gas is an example of element whereas water is a compound. Another point of distinction between an element and a compound is that when two or more elements combine to give a compound they loose their individual chemical characteristics. Hence, hydrogen and oxygen which are gases at room temperature lose their chemical identity when they form water whose properties are different from its constituents. In a mixture, each of the constituents retains its characteristic properties. For example sugar retains its characteristic sweetness even in its aqueous solution. Mixture may be homogenous or heterogeneous. Heterogeneous mixtures are those in which the mixing is not uniform and which therefore have regions of different compositions. Sand with sugar, water with gasoline and dust with air are all heterogeneous mixtures. Homogenous mixtures are those in which the mixing is uniform and which, therefore, have a constant composition throughout. Air is a gaseous mixture of primarily oxygen and nitrogen, sea water is a liquid mixture of primarily sodium chloride dissolved in water and brass is a solid mixture of copper and zinc.

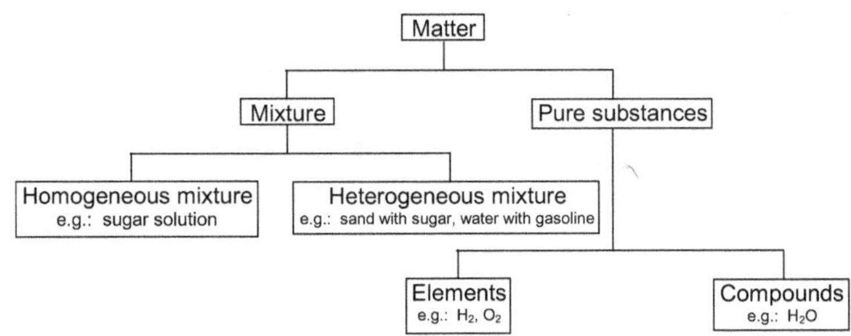

A substance is a distinct type of matter. All samples of a substance have the same properties throughout. There are two kinds of substances, elements and compounds. Thus pure water is a familiar example of a substance. All samples of pure water have the same melting and boiling point whereas sea water is not a substance; it contains both salt and other dissolved substances and water.

3   THE CONCEPTS OF ATOMS AND MOLECULES

3.1   THE ATOMS

The fact that all substances obeyed the laws of chemical combination by mass (explained later) made the scientists to speculate about the ultimate particles of matter. The most famous of these speculations is due to John Dalton.

DALTON'S ATOMIC THEORY

The main postulates of this atomic theory are

- Matter is discrete (i.e., discontinuous) and is made up of atoms. *An atom is the smallest (chemically) indivisible particle of an element, which can take part in a chemical change.*
- Atoms of the same element are identical in all respects, size, shape, structure etc. and especially mass.
- Atoms of different elements have different properties and different masses.
- Atoms can neither be created nor destroyed. So a chemical reaction is nothing but a rearrangement of atoms and the same number of atoms must be present before and after the reaction.
- A compound is formed by the union of atoms of one element with atoms of another in a fixed ratio of small whole numbers (1 : 1, 1 : 2, 2 : 3 etc).
  All the postulates of Dalton's atomic theory have been proved to be incorrect.
(i) An atom is divisible in the sense that it has got sub–atomic particles.
(ii) The existence of isotopes for most elements shows that atoms of the same element need not have the same mass. The atomic mass of an element is, in fact, a mean of the atomic masses of the different isotopes of the element.
(iii) Part of atomic mass can be destroyed and an equivalent amount of energy is released during nuclear fission.
(iv) Atoms combine in fixed integral ratios; however, there are instances where atoms combine in non–integral ratios. e.g., in zinc oxide, zinc and oxygen have not combined in exactly an integral ratio. The atomic ratio of $Zn : O = (1 + x) : 1$, where x is a very small fraction. Compounds of this kind are called *non–stoichiometric compounds or Berthollide compounds* as against compounds whose formulae are in accordance with atomic theory and Proust's law of definite proportions.
However, these aspects have not affected the basic philosophy of Dalton.

3.2 ATOMIC MASS

Dalton gave the idea of atomic mass in relative terms, that is, the average mass of one atom relative to the average mass of the other. The relative atomic masses were referred to as the *atomic masses*. It was found that 1.00 g of hydrogen combines with 8.0 g of oxygen to form water. In order to find out atomic mass of oxygen (relative to hydrogen) it is required to know the relative numbers of hydrogen and oxygen atoms in water. However during Dalton's time it was not known how many hydrogen and oxygen atoms are present in a water molecule. Now we know that a water molecule has two hydrogen and one oxygen atom. So, atomic mass of oxygen on the hydrogen scale is given by

$$\frac{\text{Relative mass of one atom of oxygen}}{\text{Relative mass of one atom of hydrogen}} = 16.$$

Thus, the atomic mass of oxygen relative to hydrogen is 16.

A scale based on oxygen, as it was considered more reactive forming a large number of compounds, eventually replaced Dalton's hydrogen based scale. Hence,

$$\text{Atomic mass of an element} = \frac{\text{mass of 1 atom of the element}}{\frac{1}{16} \times \text{mass of 1 atom of oxygen}}$$

For a universally accepted atomic mass unit in 1961, Carbon–12 isotope was selected as standard. This scale depends on measurements of atomic mass by a *mass spectrometer*. We can make accurate measurements of mass on this instrument by comparing mass of an atom with the mass of a particular atom chosen as the standard and is arbitrarily assigned a mass of exactly 12 atomic mass unit.

$$\text{Atomic mass of an element} = \frac{\text{mass of 1 atom of the element}}{\frac{1}{12} \times \text{mass of 1 atom of carbon} - 12}$$

One atomic mass unit (amu) is therefore, a mass unit equal to exactly one twelfth the mass of a carbon–12 atom. However, the new symbol 'u' (unified mass) is used now a days in place of amu.

Before moving forward, certain facts about atomic mass are summarized below:
- Atomic mass is not a mass but a number.
- Atomic mass is not absolute but relative to the mass of the standard reference element (C^{12}).
- Gram atomic mass is atomic mass expressed in grams, but it has a special significance with reference to a mole (which is discussed later).

3.3 AVERAGE ATOMIC MASS

A particular element may consist of several isotopes with different atomic masses. For such species the atomic mass calculated is the average relative atomic mass. The average relative atomic mass depends upon the isotopic composition or fractional abundance i.e. fraction of the total number of atoms that is composed of that particular isotope evaluated through mass spectrometer. Thus, the average relative atomic mass of Neon, whose fractional abundance is known can be evaluated as

$$\text{Average atomic mass} = \frac{\Sigma(\text{Isotopic molar mass} \times \text{percentage abundance})}{100}$$

Isotope	Fractional Abundance
^{20}Ne	0.9051
^{21}Ne	0.0027
^{22}Ne	0.0922

Average atomic mass of Ne = (20 × 0.9051) + (21 × 0.0027) + (22 × 0.0922) = 20.1871 u.

3.4 THE MOLECULE

Avogadro suggested that the fundamental chemical unit is not an atom but a molecule, which may be a cluster of atoms held together in some manner causing them to exist as a unit.

The term *molecule means the smallest particle of an element or a compound that can exist free and retain all its properties.*

Consider a molecule of sulphur dioxide. It has been established that it contains one atom of sulphur and two atoms of oxygen. This molecule can be split up into atoms of sulphur and oxygen. So the smallest particle of sulphur dioxide that can exist free and retain all its properties is the molecule of sulphur dioxide. A compound molecule should contain at least 2 different atoms.

The term molecule is also applied to describe the smallest particle of an element which can exist free. Thus a hydrogen molecule is proved to contain 2 atoms; when it is split up into atoms, a change in properties is observed (You may know that nascent hydrogen which may be thought of as atomic hydrogen is a more powerful reducing agent than ordinary hydrogen).

Molecules of elementary gases like hydrogen, oxygen, nitrogen, chlorine, etc., contain 2 atoms in a molecule; they are diatomic. Molecules of noble gases like helium, neon, argon, krypton and xenon are monoatomic. Molecules of phosphorus contain 4 atoms (tetratomic) while those of sulphur contain 8 atoms.

The number of atoms of an element in a molecule of the element is called its atomicity.

3.5 MOLECULAR MASS

It is the number of times a molecule is heavier than $\dfrac{1}{12}$ th the mass of an atom of C–12.

$$\text{Molecular mass} = \frac{\text{mass of one molecule}}{\dfrac{1}{12} \times \text{mass of one C} - 12 \text{ atom}}$$

- Molecular mass is not a mass but a number.
- Molecular mass is relative and not absolute.
- Molecular mass expressed in grams is called gram–molecular mass.
- Molecular mass is calculated by adding all the atomic masses of all the atoms in a molecule. Thus, the molecular mass of oxygen which contains 2 atoms in a molecule would be $(2 \times 16) = 32$. The molecular mass of carbon dioxide, which contains 1 atom of carbon and 2 atoms of oxygen would be $[12 + (2 \times 16)] = 44$. Molecular mass of sulphuric acid, which contains 2 atoms of hydrogen, 1 atom of sulphur and 4 atoms of oxygen is $[(2 \times 1) + (1 \times 32) + (4 \times 16)] = 98$.
- Molecular mass is now called relative molecular mass.

Note: The *formula mass* of a substance is the sum of the atomic masses of all atoms in a formula unit of the compound. Sodium chloride, NaCl is an ionic substance and we do not talk about its molecular mass. Formula mass of NaCl = 58.5 u (for Na = 23.0 u and Cl = 35.5 u).

<table>
<tr><td colspan="2" align="center">Key points</td></tr>
<tr><td>1.</td><td>Dalton's atomic theory considers the matter to be made up of atoms.</td></tr>
<tr><td>2.</td><td>1 amu is defined as $\dfrac{1}{12}$ th of the mass of a C^{12} atom.</td></tr>
<tr><td>3.</td><td>Average atomic mass = $\dfrac{\Sigma(\text{Isotopic atomic mass} \times \text{percentage abundance})}{100}$</td></tr>
<tr><td>4.</td><td>Molecule is the smallest particle of an element or a compound that can exist free and retain all its properties.</td></tr>
<tr><td>5.</td><td>The number of atoms of an element in a molecule is called its atomicity.</td></tr>
</table>

4   LAWS OF CHEMICAL COMBINATION

One of the most important aspects of the subject of chemistry is the study of chemical reactions. These chemical reactions take place according to certain laws which are known as laws of chemical combination. These are as follows:

1. Law of conservation of mass.
2. Law of definite proportion.
3. Law of multiple proportion.
4. Gay Lussac's law of gaseous volumes.
5. Avogadro's law.

4.1   LAW OF CONSERVATION OF MASS

The great French chemist, Antoine Laurent Lavoisier established that when combustion is carried out in a closed container ,the mass of the combustion products was exactly equal to the mass of the consumed reactants. For example, when hydrogen gas burns and combines with oxygen to yield water (H_2O), the mass of the water formed is equal to the mass of the hydrogen and oxygen consumed. In other words, ***mass is neither created nor destroyed in chemical reaction.***

Illustration 1

Question: When 4.2 g of $NaHCO_3$ is added to a solution of acetic acid (CH_3COOH) weighing 3 g, it is observed that 2.2 g of CO_2 is released into the atmosphere. The mass of CH_3COOH and H_2O left behind is found to weigh 5g. Show that these observations are in agreement with the law of conservation of mass, assuming the reactants are completely consumed.

Solution: The reaction can be expressed by

$$CH_3COOH + NaHCO_3 \longrightarrow \underbrace{CH_3COONa + H_2O}_{Residue} + CO_2 \uparrow$$

Net weight of reactants = weight of CH_3COOH + weight of $NaHCO_3$
$$= 3\,g + 4.2\,g = 7.2\,g$$
Net weight of products = weight of residue + weight of CO_2
$$= 5\,g + 2.2\,g = 7.2\,g$$
Thus, the net weight of reactants = weight of products.
Hence, the law of conservation of mass holds good.

4.2   LAW OF DEFINITE PROPORTION OR CONSTANT COMPOSITION

Further investigations in the decades following Lavoisier led the French chemist Joseph Proust formulate a second fundamental chemical principle that we now call the law of definite proportion, which states that ***a sample of pure compound, always consists of the same elements combined together in the same proportions by mass.*** For example one molecule of ammonia NH_3 always contains one atom of nitrogen and three atoms of hydrogen or 14.0 grams of nitrogen and 3.0 grams of hydrogen.

Illustration 2

Question: 6.488 g lead combines directly with 1.002 g of oxygen to form lead dioxide (PbO_2). Lead dioxide is also produced by heating lead nitrate and it was found that the percentage of oxygen present in lead dioxide is 13.38 per cent. Use these data to illustrate the law of constant composition.

Solution: To verify the law of constant composition the percentage of oxygen or lead in the lead dioxide obtained from both the experiments should be constant. So, moving stepwise, lets evaluate the percentage of oxygen in experiment 1.
In experiment 1,
Weight of lead = 6.488 g

Weight of lead dioxide = mass of lead + mass of oxygen = 6.488 + 1.002 = 7.490 g (In accordance with the law of conservation of mass)

∴   Percentage of oxygen in the dioxide thus formed

$$= \frac{\text{weight of oxygen}}{\text{weight of lead dioxide}} \times 100 \ = \ \frac{1.002}{7.490} \times 100 = 13.38\%$$

Now, the percentage of oxygen present in lead dioxide obtained from experiment 2 is 13.38 % (given).

Since, the percentage composition of oxygen in both the samples of PbO_2 is identical, the above data illustrates the law of constant composition.

4.3   LAW OF MULTIPLE PROPORTIONS

This law was studied by Dalton and may be defined as ***when two elements combine to form two or more chemical compounds, then the ratio of the mass of one of these elements, which combine with a fixed mass of the other bears a simple ratio to one another.***

For example, carbon combines with oxygen to form two compounds, namely, carbon dioxide and carbon monoxide.

$$C + \frac{1}{2}O_2 \longrightarrow CO$$

12g   16g   28g

$$C + O_2 \longrightarrow CO_2$$

12g   32g   44g

In carbon dioxide, 12 parts by weight of carbon combine with 32 parts by weight of oxygen while in carbon monoxide, 12 parts by weight of carbon combine with 16 parts by weight of oxygen. Therefore, the weights of oxygen which combine with a fixed weight of carbon (12 parts) in carbon monoxide and carbon dioxide are 16 and 32 respectively. These weights of oxygen bear a simple ratio of 16 : 32 or 1 : 2 to each other.

Illustration 3

Question: **Two oxides of a certain metal were separately heated in a current of hydrogen until constant weights were obtained. The water produced in each case was carefully collected and weighed. 2 grams of each oxide gave respectively, 0.2517 gram and 0.4526 gram of water. Show that these results establish the law of multiple proportion.**

Solution: To verify the law of multiple proportion in each case. The weight of oxygen combining with the fixed weight of the metal in the two different oxides should bear a simple ratio to one another. So, to prove this, we move stepwise as follows:

Step 1. Calculate the weight of oxygen in each oxide.

Here, we are given :

Weight of each oxide = 2.0 g

Weight of water produced in case I = 0.2517 g

Weight of water produced in case II = 0.4526 g

18 g of $H_2O \equiv$ 16 g of oxygen

i.e.   18 g of water contain oxygen = 16 g

∴   0.2517 g of water contains oxygen = $\frac{16}{18} \times 0.2517$ g = 0.2237 g

and 0.4526 g of water contains oxygen = $\frac{16}{18} \times 0.4526$ g = 0.4023 g

Step 2. Calculate the weight of oxygen which would combine with 1 g of metal in each oxide.

In case I, Weight of metal oxide = 2g and weight of oxygen = 0.2237 g

∴   Weight of metal = 2 – 0.2237 = 1.7763 g

∴   Weight of oxygen which combines with 1.7763 g of metal = 0.2237 g

 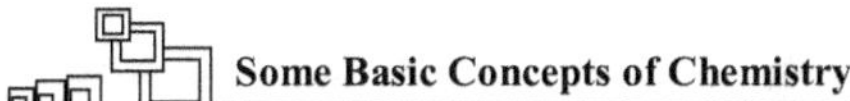 

$\therefore$ Weight of oxygen which combines with 1 g of metal = $\dfrac{0.2237}{1.7763}$ g = 0.1259 g

In case II, Weight of metal oxide = 2g and weight of oxygen = 0.4023 g

$\therefore$ Weight of metal = 2 – 0.4023 = 1.5977 g

Weight of oxygen which combines with 1.5977 g of metal = 0.4023 g

$\therefore$ Weight of oxygen which combines with 1 g of metal = $\dfrac{0.4023}{1.5977}$ g = 0.2518 g

Step 3. Compare the weights of oxygen which combine with the same weight of metal in the two oxides.

The weights of oxygen which combine with 1 g of metal in the two oxides are respectively 0.1259 g and 0.2518 g. These weights are in the ratio 0.1259 : 0.2518 or 1 : 2.

Since this is a simple ratio, so the above results establish the law of multiple proportions.

4.4 GAY LUSSAC'S LAW OF COMBINING VOLUMES

Gay Lussac investigated a large number of chemical reactions occurring in gases and as a result of his experiments ,Gay Lussac found that there exists a definite relationship among the volumes of gaseous reactants and products. Hence, he put forward a generalization known as the Gay Lussac's Law of combining volumes. This may be stated as follows *when gases react they do so in volumes which bear a simple ratio to one another and to the volumes of products, if these are also gases, provided all measurements are done under similar conditions of temperature and pressure.*

Example: One volume of hydrogen and one volume of chlorine always combine to form two volumes of hydrogenchloride.

$$H_2(g) \quad + \quad Cl_2(g) \longrightarrow 2HCl(g)$$
$$\text{1vol} \qquad\qquad \text{1vol} \qquad\qquad \text{2vol}$$

The ratio between the volumes of the reactants and the products in this reaction is simple i.e. 1:1:2. Hence, it illustrates the law of combining volumes.

4.5 AVOGADRO'S LAW

It states that equal volumes of gases at the same temperature and pressure contain equal number of molecules. It means that 1 ml of hydrogen, oxygen, ammonia, or a mixture of gases taken at the same temperature and pressure contains the same number of molecules. Avogadro's law can prove that simple elementary gas molecules like hydrogen and oxygen are diatomic.

Consider the experimental result,

1 volume of hydrogen + 1 volume of chlorine $\longrightarrow$ 2 volumes of hydrogen chloride at the same temperature and pressure.

Let 1 volume contains 'n' molecules. Then 'n' molecules of hydrogen and 'n' molecules of chlorine gives '2n' molecules of hydrogen chloride.

Canceling the common 'n', we have 1 molecule of hydrogen and 1 molecule of chlorine gives 2 molecules of hydrogen chloride.

A molecule of hydrogen chloride should contain at least 1 atom of hydrogen and 1 atom of chlorine. Two molecules of hydrogen chloride should contain at least 2 atoms of hydrogen and 2 atoms of chlorine and these should have come from 1 molecule of hydrogen and 1 molecule of chlorine respectively. Thus Avogadro's hypothesis enables us to establish that hydrogen and chlorine molecules must contain *at least 2 atoms.*

Key points

1. **Law of conservation of mass:** Mass is neither created nor destroyed in a chemical reaction.

2. **Law of definite proportion:** A sample of pure compound always consists of the same elements combined together in the same proportions by mass.

3. **Law of multiple proportion:** When two elements combine to form two or more chemical compounds, then the ratio of mass of one of these elements which combine with a fixed mass of the other bears a simple ratio to one another.

4. **Gay Lussac's law of gaseous volumes:** When gases react they do so in volumes which bear a simple ratio to one another and to the volumes of products, if these are also gases, provided all measurements are done under similar conditions of temperature and pressure.

5. **Avogadro's law:** Equal volumes of gases at the same temperature and pressure contain equal number of molecules.

5 PERCENTAGE COMPOSITION AND MOLECULAR FORMULA

A formula is a symbolic representation of a molecule of a substance, which tells us the number and kinds of atoms of various elements present in its molecule. e.g. formula of sulphuric acid is H_2SO_4 i.e. each molecule of sulphuric acid consists of two atoms of hydrogen, one atom of sulphur and four atoms of oxygen.

5.1 CALCULATION OF PERCENTAGE COMPOSITION FROM FORMULA

The percentage of any element or constituent in a compound is the number of parts by mass of that element or constituent present in 100 parts by mass of the compound. It can be determined by the following two steps

1. **Calculation of the molecular mass**

   Calculate the molecular weight of the compound from its formula by adding the atomic masses of the elements present.

2. **Calculation of the percentage composition of the constituents**

   The percentage can be calculated by using the following relation:

   $$\% \text{ of the element} = \frac{\text{No. of parts by mass of the element} \times 100}{\text{Molecular weight of the compound}}$$

Illustration 4

Question: $Fe_2(SO_4)_3$ is used in water and sewage treatment to aid the removal of suspended impurities. Calculate the mass percentage of iron, sulphur and oxygen in this compound.

Solution: **Step 1:**

Molecular weight of $Fe_2(SO_4)_3 = (56 \times 2) + (32 \times 3) + (16 \times 12) = 400$

Step 2:

$$\% \text{ of Fe} = \frac{\text{Numer of parts by weight of Fe}}{\text{Molecular weight of } Fe_2(SO_4)_3} \times 100$$

$$= \frac{56 \times 2}{400} \times 100 = \textbf{28\%.}$$

$$\% \text{ of S} = \frac{\text{Numer of parts by weight of S}}{\text{Molecular weight of } Fe_2(SO_4)_3} \times 100$$

$$= \frac{32 \times 3}{400} \times 100 = \textbf{24\%.}$$

$$\% \text{ of O} = \frac{\text{Numer of parts by weight of O}}{\text{Molecular weight of } Fe_2(SO_4)_3} \times 100$$

$$= \frac{16 \times 12}{400} \times 100 = \textbf{48\%.}$$

5.2 EMPIRICAL AND MOLECULAR FORMULA

Whereas, molecular formula of the compound represents the true formula of a compound; the empirical formula of a compound is the simplest formula that shows the ratio of the number of atoms of each kind in the compound. For example, the molecular formula of hydrogen peroxide is H_2O_2, showing that a molecule of hydrogen peroxide consists of two hydrogen atoms and two oxygen atoms or the ratio of number of hydrogen atoms to that of oxygen atoms is 2 : 2 or 1 : 1. Therefore, the simplest or empirical formula for hydrogen peroxide is HO.

5.2.1 Calculation of the empirical formula

The empirical formula of a chemical compound can be deduced from a knowledge of the

(a) percentage composition of different elements.

(b) atomic masses of the elements.

1. **Calculation of the relative number of atoms or atomic ratio**

   Divide the percentage of each element by its atomic mass. This gives the relative number of atoms or the atomic ratio of the various elements present in one molecule of the compound.

$$\text{Atomic ratio} = \frac{\text{Percentage of an element}}{\text{Atomic mass of the same element}}.$$

2. **Evaluating the simplest atomic ratio**

   Divide the atomic ratio obtained in step 1 by the smallest quotient or the least value from amongst the values obtained for each element. This gives the simplest atomic ratio.

3. **Calculate the simplest whole number ratio**

   The simplest atomic ratios as calculated in step 2 are generally whole numbers.

   If they are not, then

   (a) round off the values to the nearest whole number.

   (b) multiply all the simplest atomic ratios by a suitable integer.

4. **Deducing the empirical formula**

   Write the symbols of the various elements side by side. Now insert the numerical value of the simplest whole number ratio of each element as obtained in step 3 at the lower right hand corner of each symbol. This gives the empirical formula of the compound.

Illustration 5

Question: An inorganic salt gave the following percentage composition: Na = 29.11%, S = 40.51% and O = 30.38%. Calculate the empirical formula of the salt.

Solution: Calculation of empirical formula.

Element	Symbol	% of element	At. mass of element	Relative no. of atoms = $\dfrac{\text{Percentage}}{\text{Atomic mass}}$	Simplest atomic ratio	Simplest whole number atomic ratio
Sodium	Na	29.11	23	$\dfrac{29.11}{23} = 1.266$	$\dfrac{1.266}{1.266} = 1$	2
Sulphur	S	40.51	32	$\dfrac{40.51}{32} = 1.266$	$\dfrac{1.266}{1.266} = 1$	2
Oxygen	O	30.38	16	$\dfrac{30.38}{16} = 1.898$	$\dfrac{1.898}{1.266} = 1.49$ $\cong 1.5$	3

Thus, the empirical formula is $Na_2S_2O_3$.

5.2.2 Calculation of the molecular formula

The molecular formula of a compound can be deduced from its

(a) empirical formula

(b) molecular mass

The determination of molecular formula involves the following steps :

(i) Calculation of the empirical formula from its percentage composition.

(ii) Calculation of empirical formula mass by adding the atomic masses of all the atoms present in the empirical formula.

(iii) Determination of the molecular mass of the compound from the given data.

(iv) Determination of the value of 'n' by using the relation,

$$n = \frac{\text{Molecular mass}}{\text{Empirical formula mass}}, \text{ where n is any integer such as } 1,2,3\ldots\ldots \text{ etc.}$$

(v) Determination of the molecular formula by using the relation

Molecular formula = n × empirical formula.

6 STOICHIOMETRY

Chemical stoichiometry deals with the determination of quantities of reactants or products of a chemical reaction. The word "stoichiometry" is derived from greek word *"stoicheion"* meaning element and *"metron"* meaning measure.

6.1 THE MOLE

The concept of amount of a substance is confined to the chemical measurements. The amount of substance of a system is proportional to the number of elementary entities (which may be atoms or molecules or ions or specified group of such particles) of that substance present in the system.

Let us take elements Ag, Mg and Hg with masses equal to their atomic masses in grams, and then to our surprise, each element contains equal number of atoms. This is not only limited to atoms but also applicable to the molecules. For example, if we have molecules like CO_2, NO_2 and SO_2 with masses equal to their molecular masses in grams, then they would also contain equal number of molecules. This specified number of atoms or molecules is referred to as a "mole".

Thus, a system containing a specified number (6.023×10^{23}) of elementary entities is said to contain 1 mole of the entities. Thus 1 mole of an iron sample means that the sample contains 6.023×10^{23} atoms of iron. Similarly, 1 mole of NaCl crystal contains 6.023×10^{23} ion pairs (Na^+Cl^-).

This specific number 6.023×10^{23} elementary entities is called Avogadro number (N_{AV}). The SI unit for amount of substance is the mole. *One mole is defined as the amount of a substance that contains as many entities (atoms, molecules or other particles) as there are in exactly 12 g of ^{12}C isotope.*

$$\text{Number of moles of species} = \frac{\text{No. of atoms / molecules of that species}}{\text{Avogadro Number}}$$

The mass of specific number (6.023×10^{23}) of elementary entities is equal to atomic mass for atoms and molecular mass for molecules.

Let 'M' g/mole be the molecular mass of a species. Thus 'M' g be the mass of 1 mole (equal to the mass of 6.023×10^{23} molecules) of the species. Then, 'x' g of the species contain $\left(\frac{1}{M} \times x\right)$ mole. Hence

$$\text{Number of moles of a species} = \frac{\text{mass taken (grams)}}{\text{Atomic or molecular mass (g/mole)}} = \frac{w}{M}$$

It is also known that one mole of a gas at STP occupies a volume of 22.4 litres. Thus, if a gas occupies 'x' L at STP, then the number of moles of the gas can be calculated by dividing the actual volume occupied by the gas at STP with the volume occupied by 1 mole of the gas at STP.

$$\text{Thus, number of moles of a gas} = \frac{\text{Volume occupied by gas at STP}}{\text{Volume occupied by 1 mole of the gas at STP}}.$$

The volume of gas and the number of moles of gas at temperature and pressure other than the STP can be related by ideal gas equation, $PV = nRT$.

Illustration 6

Question: Calculate the number of atoms in each of the following
   (i) **52 moles of Ar**
   (ii) **52 u of He**
   (iii) **52 g of He**

Solution: (i) 1 mole of Ar contains 6.023×10^{23} atoms

$\therefore$ 52 mole of Ar contains atoms

$$= 52 \times 6.023 \times 10^{23}$$
$$= 3.132 \times 10^{25} \text{ atoms.}$$

(ii) 1 atom of He contains 4 u

$$\therefore \quad 52 \text{ u of He contains} = \frac{52}{4} \times 1 = 13 \text{ atoms.}$$

(iii) 1 mol of He $\equiv$ 4 g $= 6.023 \times 10^{23}$ atoms

$$\therefore 52 \text{ g of He contains atoms} = \frac{52 \text{ g}}{4 \text{ g}} \times 6.023 \times 10^{23} = \mathbf{7.8299 \times 10^{24} \text{ atoms.}}$$

6.2 BALANCING A CHEMICAL EQUATION

According to the law of conservation of mass, a balanced chemical equation has the same number of atoms of each element on both sides of the equation. Many chemical equations can be balanced by trial and error. Let us take the reactions of a few metals and non–metals with oxygen to give oxides

$$4Fe(s) + 3O_2(g) \longrightarrow 2Fe_2O_3(s) \qquad \text{(a) balanced equation}$$
$$2Mg(s) + O_2(g) \longrightarrow 2MgO(s) \qquad \text{(b) balanced equation}$$
$$P_4(s) + O_2(g) \longrightarrow P_4O_{10}(s) \qquad \text{(c) unbalanced equation}$$

Equations (a) and (b) are balanced since there are same number of metal and oxygen atoms on each side of equations. However, equation (c) is not balanced. In this equation, phosphorus atoms are balanced but not the oxygen atoms. To balance it, we must place the coefficient 5 on the left of oxygen on the left side of the equation to balance the oxygen atoms appearing on the right side of the equation.

$$P_4(s) + 5O_2(g) \longrightarrow P_4O_{10}(s) \qquad \text{balanced equation}$$

Now let us take combustion of propane, C_3H_8. This equation can be balanced in steps.

Step 1. Write down the correct formulae of reactants and products. Here propane and oxygen are reactants and carbon dioxide and water are products.

$$C_3H_8(g) + O_2(g) \longrightarrow CO_2(g) + H_2O(l) \qquad \text{unbalanced equation}$$

Step 2. Balance the number of C atoms: Since 3 carbon atoms are in the reactant, therefore, three CO_2 molecules are required on the right side.

$$C_3H_8(g) + O_2(g) \longrightarrow 3CO_2(g) + H_2O(l) \qquad \text{unbalanced equation}$$

Step 3. Balance the number of H atoms: Since on the left there are 8 hydrogen atoms in the reactants however, each molecule of water has two hydrogen atoms, so four molecules of water will be required for eight hydrogen atoms on the right side.

$$C_3H_8(g) + O_2(g) \longrightarrow 3CO_2(g) + 4H_2O(l) \qquad \text{unbalanced equation}$$

Step 4. Balance the number of O atoms: There are ten oxygen atoms on the right side ($3 \times 2 = 6$ in CO_2 and $4 \times 1 = 4$ in H_2O). Therefore, five O_2 molecules are needed to supply the required ten oxygen atoms.

$$C_3H_8(g) + 5O_2(g) \longrightarrow 3CO_2(g) + 4H_2O(l)$$

Step 5. Verify that the number of atoms of each element is balanced in the final equation. The equation shows three carbon atoms, eight hydrogen atoms and ten oxygen atoms on each side.

All equations that have correct formulae for all reactants and products can be balanced. Always remember that subscripts in formulae of reactants and products cannot be changed to balance an equation.

6.3 QUANTITATIVE INFORMATION FROM A BALANCED CHEMICAL EQUATION

Let us now consider a balanced chemical equation as

$$MnO_2 + 4HCl \longrightarrow MnCl_2 + 2H_2O + Cl_2$$

The quantitative information drawn from this balanced chemical equation is

(a) The molar ratio in which the two reactants (MnO_2 and HCl) are reacting is $1:4$.

(b) The molar ratio between any two products can also be known i.e. moles of H_2O produced would be double the moles of $MnCl_2$ produced.

(c) The initial moles of MnO_2 and HCl to be taken in vessel for the reaction to occur not necessarily be 1 and 4 respectively (or in the molar ratio of $1:4$).

(d) We can start reaction with MnO_2 and HCl taken in any molar ratio, but moles of the two reacting will always be in the molar ratio of $1:4$.

(e) The balanced chemical equation should follow the law of conservation of mass.

6.4. STOICHIOMETRIC CALCULATIONS

Let us consider the same chemical system as considered above with initial composition (in terms of mole) as $n^{\circ}_{MnO_2}, n^{\circ}_{HCl}, n^{\circ}_{MnCl_2}, n^{\circ}_{H_2O}$, and $n^{\circ}_{Cl_2}$. Let the n°_{HCl} is four times that of $n^{\circ}_{MnO_2}$.

When the reaction occurs, these mole numbers change as the reaction progresses. The mole numbers of the various species do not change independently but the changes are related by the stoichiometric coefficients in the chemical equation. Let after time 't' from the commencement of the reaction, the moles of MnO_2 reacting be 'x', then the moles of HCl reacting in the same time interval be '$4x$' since MnO_2 and HCl react in the molar ratio of $1:4$.

Thus, after time t, the composition of the system would be

$$n_{MnO_2} = n^{\circ}_{MnO_2} - x$$

$$n_{HCl} = n^{\circ}_{HCl} - 4x$$

$$n_{MnCl_2} = n^{\circ}_{MnCl_2} + x$$

$$n_{H_2O} = n^{\circ}_{H_2O} + 2x$$

$$n_{Cl_2} = n^{\circ}_{Cl_2} + x$$

The algebric signs, $-$ and $+$ indicates that the reactants are consumed and the products are produced.

In general, mole numbers of various species at any time would be given as

$$n_t = n_i^{\circ} + v_i^{\circ} x$$

where n_i° is the initial amount, x is the degree of advancement and v_i is the stoichiometric coefficient which will be given a negative sign for the reactants and a positive sign for the products.

After long time interval from the commencement of reaction i.e. after infinite time, i.e., when the reaction is 100% complete, the composition of the system would be

$$n_{MnO_2} = 0, \quad n_{HCl} = 0$$

$$n_{MnCl_2} = n^{\circ}_{MnCl_2} + n^{\circ}_{MnO_2} = n^{\circ}_{MnCl_2} + \frac{n^{\circ}_{HCl}}{4}$$

$$n_{H_2O} = n^{\circ}_{H_2O} + 2n^{\circ}_{MnO_2} = n^{\circ}_{H_2O} + \frac{n^{\circ}_{HCl}}{2}$$

$$n_{Cl_2} = n^{\circ}_{Cl_2} + n^{\circ}_{MnO_2} = n^{\circ}_{Cl_2} + \frac{n^{\circ}_{HCl}}{4}$$

6.5   THE LIMITING REAGENT

Let the initial moles of MnO_2 and HCl be $n^{\circ}_{MnO_2}$ and n°_{HCl} respectively and $n^{\circ}_{HCl} \neq 4n^{\circ}_{MnO_2}$.

Thus, in the given chemical reaction, after infinite time, one of the reactant will be completely consumed while the other would be left in excess. Thus, the reactant which is completely consumed when a reaction goes to completion and which decides the yield of the product is called the limiting reagent.

For example, if in the given case $n^{\circ}_{HCl} > 4n^{\circ}_{MnO_2}$, and there is no $MnCl_2$ and H_2O in the beginning, then

	MnO_2	+	4HCl	$\longrightarrow$	$MnCl_2$	+	Cl_2	+	$2H_2O$
Initially, t = 0	$n^{\circ}_{MnO_2}$		n°_{HCl}		0		0		0
At t = ∞	0		$n^{\circ}_{HCl} - 4n^{\circ}_{MnO_2}$		$n^{\circ}_{MnO_2}$		$n^{\circ}_{MnO_2}$		$2n^{\circ}_{MnO_2}$

Thus, MnO_2 is the limiting reagent and the yield of all the products is governed by the amount of MnO_2 taken initially.

Similarly, if in the given case $n^{\circ}_{HCl} < 4n^{\circ}_{MnO_2}$ and no $MnCl_2$, Cl_2 and H_2O are present initially, then

	MnO_2	+	4HCl	$\longrightarrow$	$MnCl_2$	+	Cl_2	+	$2H_2O$
Initially, t = 0	$n^{\circ}_{MnO_2}$		n°_{HCl}		0		0		0
t = ∞	$n^{\circ}_{MnO_2} - \dfrac{n^{\circ}_{HCl}}{4}$		0		$\dfrac{n^{\circ}_{HCl}}{4}$		$\dfrac{n^{\circ}_{HCl}}{4}$		$\dfrac{n^{\circ}_{HCl}}{2}$

Here, HCl would become the limiting reagent and the products yield are decided by the amount of HCl taken initially.

6.6   ANALYSIS BASED ON MASS AND VOLUME RELATIONSHIPS

This analysis section is broadly classified into three heads.

(a)   Mass–mass relationship

(b)   Mass–volume relationship and

(c)   Volume–volume relationship

6.6.1   Mass–mass Relationship

This relates the mass of a species (reactant or product) with the mass of another species (reactant or product) involved in a chemical reaction.

Let us consider a chemical reaction,

$$CaCO_3(s) \xrightarrow{\Delta} CaO(s) + CO_2(g).$$

Let the mass of $CaCO_3$ taken be 'x' g and we want to calculate the mass of CaO obtained by heating 'x' g $CaCO_3$. Then the moles of $CaCO_3$ taken would be $\dfrac{x}{M_1}$ (where M_1 represents the molar mass of $CaCO_3$). According to the balanced reaction, the molar ratio of $CaCO_3$ and CaO is $1:1$, so same number of moles $\left(\dfrac{x}{M_1}\right)$ of CaO would be formed. Now for converting the moles of CaO into mass of CaO obtained, we need to multiply the moles of CaO with the molar mass of CaO.

Let the molar mass of CaO be M_2, so the mass of CaO obtained by heating 'x' g of $CaCO_3$ would be $\left(\dfrac{x}{M_1}\times M_2\right)$ g.

6.6.2 Mass–volume Relationship

This establishes the relationship between the mass of a species (reactant or product) and the volume of a gaseous species (reactant or product) involved in a chemical reaction.

Let us take 'x' g of $CaCO_3$ in a vessel of capacity 'V' L and the vessel is heated so that $CaCO_3$ decomposes as

$$CaCO_3(s) \xrightarrow{\Delta} CaO(s) + CO_2(g)$$

We want to find out the volume of CO_2 evolved at STP by heating 'x' g of $CaCO_3$. Then

$$\text{Moles of } CaCO_3 = \frac{x}{M_1}$$

$$\text{Moles of } CO_2 \text{ evolved} = \frac{x}{M_1} \quad (\text{since molar ratio of } CaCO_3 \text{ and } CO_2 \text{ is } 1:1)$$

$$\therefore \text{ Volume of } CO_2 \text{ evolved at STP} = \left(\frac{x}{M_1}\times 22.4\right) L$$

But, if the volume of CO_2 evolved is to be calculated at pressure 'P' atm and temperature 'T' K.

Then, Volume of CO_2 evolved at pressure 'P' and temperature 'T' $= \dfrac{x}{M_1}\times\dfrac{RT}{P}$ (Using $PV = nRT$)

Illustration 7

Question: Oxygen is prepared by catalytic decomposition of potassium chlorate ($KClO_3$). Decomposition of potassium chlorate gives potassium chloride (KCl) and oxygen (O_2). How many moles and how many grams of $KClO_3$ are required to produce 2.4 mole O_2? ($M_{KClO_3} = 122.5 \text{ g/mole}$)

Solution: Decomposition of $KClO_3$ takes place as

$$2KClO_3(s) \longrightarrow 2KCl(s) + 3O_2(g)$$

2 mole $KClO_3$ gives 3 mole of O_2

$\because$ 3 mole O_2 is formed by 2 mole of $KClO_3$.

$\because$ 2.4 mole O_2 will be formed by $\left(\dfrac{2}{3}\times 2.4\right)$ mole $KClO_3$ = 1.6 mole $KClO_3$.

Mass of $KClO_3$ = Number of moles × Molar mass = $1.6 \times 122.5 = 196$ g.

Illustration 8

Question: If 20 g of $CaCO_3$ is treated with 20 g of HCl, how many grams of CO_2 can be generated according to the following equation?

$$CaCO_3(s) + 2HCl(aq) \longrightarrow CaCl_2(aq) + H_2O(l) + CO_2(g)$$

Solution:

$$CaCO_3(s) + 2HCl(aq) \longrightarrow CaCl_2(aq) + H_2O(l) + CO_2(g)$$

1 mol	2 mol		1 mol
100 g	73 g		44 g

Let $CaCO_3(s)$ be completely consumed in the reaction.

$\therefore$ 100 g $CaCO_3$ gives 44 g CO_2.

$$\therefore \quad 20 \text{ g CaCO}_3 \text{ will give } \frac{44}{100} \times 20 \text{ g CO}_2 = 8.8 \text{ g CO}_2.$$

Let HCl be completely consumed

$\because$ 73 g HCl give 44 g CO_2

$$\therefore \quad 20 \text{ g HCl will give } \frac{44}{73} \times 20 \text{ g CO}_2 = 12.054 \text{ g CO}_2.$$

Since, $CaCO_3$ gives least amount of product CO_2, hence $CaCO_3$ is the limiting reactant.

Illustration 9

Question: **For the reaction,**

$$CaO + 2HCl \longrightarrow CaCl_2 + H_2O$$

1.23 g of CaO is reacted with excess of hydrochloric acid and 1.85 g of $CaCl_2$ is formed. What is the percent yield?

$$\left(\% \text{ yield} = \frac{\text{mass of the product produced actually}}{\text{mass of the product produced theoretically}} \times 100 \right)$$

Solution: The balanced equation is

$$\begin{array}{ccccccc} CaO & + & 2HCl & \longrightarrow & CaCl_2 & + & H_2O \\ 1 \text{ mol} & & & & 1 \text{ mol} \\ 56 \text{ g} & & & & 111 \text{g} \end{array}$$

56 g of CaO produce $CaCl_2$ = 111 g

$$1.23 \text{ g of CaO produce CaCl}_2 = \frac{111}{56} \times 1.23 = 2.438$$

Thus, theoretical yield = 2.438 g

Actual yield = 1.85 g

$$\text{Percent yield} = \frac{1.85}{2.438} \times 100 = 75.88\%.$$

6.6.3 Volume–volume Relationship

This relationship deals with the volume of a gaseous species (reactant or product) with the volume of another gaseous species (reactant or product) involved in a chemical reaction.

Let us consider the reaction, $N_2(g) + 3H_2(g) \longrightarrow 2NH_3(g)$. We are given '$x$' L of N_2 at pressure 'P' atm and temperature 'T' K and we want to know the volume of H_2 required to react with it at another pressure P' atm and temperature T' K, then

$$\text{Moles of N}_2 = \frac{Px}{RT}$$

$$\text{Moles of H}_2 \text{ required} = \frac{3 \times P \times x}{RT}$$

$\therefore$ Volume of H_2 required at pressure P' atm and temperature T' K

$$= \frac{3 \times P \times x \times RT'}{RT \times P'} = \left(\frac{3x \times PT'}{P'T} \right) L$$

Illustration 10

Question: **1 litre mixture of CO and CO_2 is taken. This is passed through a tube containing red hot charcoal. The volume now becomes 1.6 litre. The volumes are measured under the same conditions. Find the composition of mixture by volume.**

Solution: Let there be 'x' ml of CO in the mixture. Hence there will be $(1000 - x)$ml CO_2. The reaction of CO_2 with red hot charcoal may be given as,

$$\begin{array}{ccccc} CO_2(g) & + & C(s) & \longrightarrow & 2CO(g) \\ 1000 - x & & & \\ - & & & & 2000 - 2x \end{array}$$

Total volume of the gas becomes = $x + 2(1000 - x)$

$$x + 2000 - 2x = 1600$$
$$x = 400 \text{ ml}$$

$\therefore$ Volume of CO = 400 ml

and volume of CO_2 = 600 ml.

7 CONCENTRATIONJ OF SOLUTION

A solution is defined as a homogenous mixture of two or more chemically non-reacting substances, the relative amount of which can be varied upto a certain limit. If a solution consists of only two components it is called a binary solution. The component present in smaller amount is called the solute while, the other present in larger amount is called the solvent.

The concentration of a solution can be expressed in a number of ways as follows:

1. Mass percent or weight percent (w / w%) 2. Mole fraction
3. Molarity 4. Molality

7.1 MASS PERCENT

It is obtained by using the following relation: Mass percent = $\dfrac{\text{Mass of solute}}{\text{Mass of solution}} \times 100$

7.2 MOLE FRACTION

It is the ratio of number of moles of a particular component to the total number of moles of the solution. If a substance 'A' dissolves in substance 'B' and their number of moles are n_A and n_B respectively; then the mole fractions of A and B are given as

$$\text{Mole fraction of A} = \frac{\text{Number of moles of A}}{\text{Number of moles of solution}}$$

$$= \frac{n_A}{n_A + n_B}$$

$$\text{Mole fraction of B} = \frac{\text{Number of moles of B}}{\text{Number of moles of solution}}$$

$$= \frac{n_B}{n_A + n_B}$$

7.3 MOLARITY (M)

It is defined as the number of moles of solute present in one litre of the solution.

$$\text{Molarity (M)} = \frac{\text{number of moles of solute}}{\text{Volume of solution (in litres)}}$$

Let the weight of solute be 'w' g, molar mass of solute be 'M_1' g/mol and the volume of solution be 'V' litre.

Hence, number of moles of solute = $\dfrac{\text{weight of solute}}{\text{Atomic or molar mass of solute}} = \dfrac{w}{M_1}$

$\therefore \quad M = \dfrac{w}{M_1} \times \dfrac{1}{V \text{(in litres)}}$

$\therefore \quad$ **Number of moles of solute** $= \dfrac{w}{M_1}$ **= M × V (in litres)**

Note: When a solution is diluted, the moles of solute donot change but molarity changes. On taking out a small volume of solution from a larger volume, the molarity of solution donot change but moles change proportionately.

7.4 MOLALITY (m)

It is defined as the number of moles of solute present in 1 kg of solvent. It is denoted by 'm'.

$$\text{Molality (m)} = \frac{\text{number of moles of solute}}{\text{mass of the solvent (in kg)}}$$

Illustration 11

Question: A solution of oxalic acid $C_2H_2O_4.2H_2O$ is prepared by dissolving 0.63 g of the acid in 250 cm³ of the solution. Calculate molarity of the solution.

Solution: Molar mass of oxalic acid = 126 g/mol.

$\therefore$ 250 cm³ or $\dfrac{250}{1000}$ L = 0.25 L of the solution contains 0.63 g oxalic acid.

$\therefore$ Molarity of the solution = $\dfrac{0.63}{126} \times \dfrac{1}{0.25}$ = 0.02 M

Illustration 12

Question: Calculate the molarity of H_2O in pure water. (density H_2O = 1 g/cm³)

Solution: 1 L of pure water = 1000 g (assuming density =1.0 g/cm³)

$\therefore$ Number of moles in 1 L of pure water = $\dfrac{1000}{18}$ = 55.55.

Key points

Adding a solvent to a solution, a process known as dilution, decreases the concentration (molarity) of the solution without changing the total moles of solute present in the solution.

EXERCISE

1. A welding fuel gas contains carbon and hydrogen only. Burning a small sample of it in oxygen gives 3.38 g of carbon dioxide, 0.690 g of water and no other products. A volume of 10.0 L (measured at STP) of this welding gas is found to weight 11.6 g. Calculate (i) empirical formula. (ii) molar mass of the gas (iii) molecular formula.

2. From the following reaction sequence,
$$CaC_2 + H_2O \longrightarrow CaO + C_2H_2$$
$$C_2H_2 + H_2 \longrightarrow C_2H_4$$
$$nC_2H_4 \longrightarrow (C_2H_4)_n$$
Calculate the mass of polyethylene which can be produced from 10 kg of CaC_2.

3. If 6.3 g of $NaHCO_3$ are added to 15.0 g CH_3COOH solution. What is the mass of CO_2 released in the atmosphere if the following reaction is known to take place?
$$CH_3COOH + NaHCO_3 \longrightarrow CH_3COONa + CO_2 + H_2O$$

4. Three atoms of magnesium combine with 2 atoms of nitrogen. What will be the weight of magnesium which combines with 1.86 g of nitrogen? The reaction occurring is as follows
$$3Mg + N_2 \longrightarrow Mg_3N_2$$

5. Calculate the total number of electrons present in 18 ml of water. Given: density of water = 1g/ml.

6. Find the ratio of the number of molecules contained in 1 g of NH_3 and 1 g of N_2?

7. Calculate the total number of atoms is 0.5 mole of $K_2Cr_2O_7$.

8. A sample of potato starch was ground in a ball mill to give a starch like molecule of lower molecular weight. The product analysed 0.086% phosphorus. If each molecule is assumed to contain one atom of phosphorus, what is the molecular weight of the material?

9. Equal masses of Zn metal and iodine are mixed together and the iodine is converted to ZnI_2. What fraction by mass of the original zinc remains unreacted? (M_{zn} = 65, M_I = 127)

10. 1.6 g of an oxide of iron, on heating in a stream of hydrogen gas, completely converted to 1.12 g of iron. Find the empirical formula of the oxide. (Atomic mass: Fe = 56)

11. Calculate the number of oxalic acid molecules in 100 ml of 0.01 M oxalic acid solution.

12. How many milliliters of 0.5 M H_2SO_4 are needed to dissolve 0.5 g of copper(II) carbonate? The following reaction takes place: $H_2SO_4 + CuCO_3 \longrightarrow CuSO_4 + H_2CO_3$.

13. Two acids H_2SO_4 and H_3PO_4 are neutralized separately by the same number of moles of an alkali when sulphate and dihydrogen orthophosphate are formed respectively. Find the ratio of the masses of H_2SO_4 and H_3PO_4 taken.
$$H_2SO_4 + 2NaOH \longrightarrow Na_2SO_4 + 2H_2O$$
$$H_3PO_4 + NaOH \longrightarrow NaH_2PO_4 + H_2O$$

14. 10 ml of HCl solution gave 0.1435 g of AgCl when treated with excess of $AgNO_3$. Find the molarity of the acid solution.

15. Calculate the weight of FeO produced from 2 g VO and 5.75 g of Fe_2O_3. Also report the limiting reagent.

$$2VO + 3Fe_2O_3 \longrightarrow 6FeO + V_2O_5$$

(Molecular mass of VO = 67, Fe_2O_3 = 160, FeO = 72)

16. 250 ml of x M solution and 500 ml of y M solution of a solute A are mixed and diluted to 2 litre to produce a final concentration of 1.6 M. If $x : y$ = 5 : 4. Calculate x and y.

17. In a process for producing acetic acid, oxygen gas is bubbled into acetaldehyde under pressure at 60°C in presence of a catalyst.

$$2CH_3CHO + O_2 \longrightarrow 2CH_3COOH$$

In a laboratory test of this reaction, 20 g of CH_3CHO and 10 g of O_2 were put into a reaction vessel.

(a) How many grams of CH_3COOH can be produced?

(b) How many grams of the excess reactant remain after the reaction is complete?

18. Find out the weight of calcium carbonate that must be decomposed to produce sufficient quantity of carbon dioxide to convert 10.6 g of sodium carbonate completely into sodium bicarbonate.

$$CaCO_3 \xrightarrow{\Delta} CaO + CO_2$$
$$Na_2CO_3 + CO_2 + H_2O \longrightarrow 2NaHCO_3$$

19. A mixture of aluminium and zinc weighing 1.67 g was completely dissolved in acid. 1.69 litre of hydrogen measured at 0^0C and 1 atm pressure was evolved. What was the weight of aluminium in the mixture.

$$Al + 3H^+ \longrightarrow Al^{3+} + \frac{3}{2}H_2$$
$$Zn + 2H^+ \longrightarrow Zn^{2+} + H_2$$

(Atomic mass of Al = 27, Zn = 65.4)

20. Chlorine gas can be produced in the laboratory by the reaction,

$$K_2Cr_2O_7 + 14HCl \longrightarrow 2KCl + 2CrCl_3 + 7H_2O + 3Cl_2.$$

If a 61.3 g sample that is 96% $K_2Cr_2O_7$ is allowed to react with 320 ml of hydrochloric acid solution having a density 1.15 g mL^{-1} and containing 30% HCl by mass, what mass of Cl_2 is generated? (Atomic masses: Cl = 35.5, K = 39, Cr = 52)

ANSWERS TO EXERCISE

1. CH, 26, C_2H_2

2. 4375 g

3. 3.3 g

4. 4.78 g

5. 6.023×10^{24} electrons

6. 28 : 17

7. 3.31×10^{24}

8. 3.6×10^4 amu / molecule

9. 0.744

10. Fe_2O_3

11. 6.023×10^{20} molecules

12. 8.1 ml

13. 1 : 2

14. 0.1 M

15. 5.17 g, Fe_2O_3

16. $x = 4.9$ and $y = 3.9$

17. 27.27 g, 2.73 g of O_2

18. 10 g

19. 1.26 g

20. 42.6 g

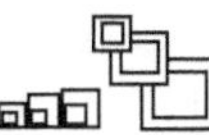

Single Correct Answer Type

1. A student performs a titration with different burettes and finds titre values of 25.2 mL, 25.25 mL, and 25.0mL. The number of significant figures in the average titre value is

   1) 1
   2) 2
   3) 3
   4) 4

2. The correctly reported answer of the addition of 4.523, 2.3 and 6.24 will have significant figures
   1) Two
   2) Three
   3) Four
   4) Five

3. The least count of an instrument is 0.01 cm. Taking all precautions, the most possible error in the measurement can be
   1) 0.005 cm
   2) 0.01 cm
   3) 0.0001 cm
   4) 0.1 cm

4. Which one of the following set of units represents the smallest and largest amount of energy respectively?
   1) J and erg
   2) erg and cal
   3) Cal and eV
   4) L-atm and J
   5) eV and L-atm

5. The value of amu is which of the following?

   1) 1.57×10^{-24} kg
   2) 1.66×10^{-24} kg
   3) 1.99×10^{-23} kg
   4) 1.66×10^{-27} kg

6. The mass of 11.2 L of ammonia gas at STP is

   1) 8.5 g
   2) 85 g
   3) 17 g
   4) 1.7 g
   5) 4.25 g

7. Law of multiple proportions is illustrated by one of the following pairs
   1) H_2S and SO_2
   2) NH_3 and NO_2
   3) Na_2S and Na_2O
   4) BeO and $BeCl_2$
   5) N_2O and NO

8. The number of hydrogen atoms present in 25.6 g of sucrose($C_{12}H_{22}O_{11}$) which has a molar mass of 342.3 g is
   1) 22×10^{23}
   2) 9.91×10^{23}
   3) 11×10^{23}
   4) 44×10^{23} H atoms

9. 80 g of oxygen contains as many atoms as in

   1) 80 g of hydrogen
   2) 1 g of hydrogen
   3) 10 g of hydrogen
   4) 5 g of hydrogen

10. Gram molecular volume of oxygen at STP is

    1) 3200 cm^3
    2) 5600 cm^3
    3) 22400 cm^3
    4) 11200 cm^3

11. How many H-atoms are present in 0.046 g of ethanol?
    1) 6×10^{20}
    2) 1.2×10^{21}
    3) 3×10^{21}
    4) 3.6×10^{21}

12. Which has maximum number of atoms?

    1) 2.0 mol of S_8
    2) 6.0 mol of S
    3) 5.5 mol of SO_2
    4) 4.48 L of CO_2 at 5TP

13. A gas has a vapour density 11.2. The volume occupied by 1g of the gas at NTP is

    1) 1 L
    2) 11.2 L
    3) 22.4 L
    4) 4 L

14. The number of atoms in 4.25 g of NH_3 is approximately
   1) 6×10^{23}
   2) 2×10^{23}
   3) 1.5×10^{23}
   4) 1×10^{23}

15. 0.1 mole of a carbohydrate with empirical formula CH_2O contains 1 g of hydrogen. What is its molecular formula?
   1) $C_5H_{10}O_5$
   2) $C_6H_{12}O_6$
   3) $C_4H_8O_4$
   4) $C_3H_6O_3$
   5) $C_2H_4O_2$

16. Law of constant composition is same as the law of
   1) Conservation of mass
   2) Conservation of energy
   3) Multiple proportion
   4) Definite proportion

17. One mole of CO_2 contains
   1) 3 g atoms of CO_2
   2) 18.1×10^{23} molecules of CO_2
   3) 6.02×10^{23} atoms of O
   4) 6.02×10^{23} atoms of C

18. The number of gram molecules of chlorine in 6.02×10^{25} hydrogen chloride molecules is
   1) 10
   2) 100
   3) 50
   4) 5

19. Which has maximum number of atoms?
   1) 24 g of C
   2) 56 g of Fe
   3) 26 g of Al
   4) 108 g of Ag

20. The number of formula units of calcium fluoride, CaF_2 present in 146.4 g of CaF_2 (the molar mass of CaF_2 is 78.08 g/mol) is
   1) $1.129 \times 10^{24} CaF_2$
   2) $1.146 \times 10^{24} CaF_2$
   3) $7.808 \times 10^{24} CaF_2$
   4) $1.877 \times 10^{24} CaF_2$

21. How many moles of $Al_2(SO_4)_3$ would be in 50 g of the substance?
   1) 0.083 mol
   2) 0.952 mol
   3) 0.481 mol
   4) 0.140 mol

22. 1 L oxygen gas at STP will weigh
   1) 1.43 g
   2) 2.24 g
   3) 11.2 g
   4) 22.4 g

23. Which has the highest weight?
   1) $1 \, m^3$ of water
   2) A normal adult man
   3) 10 L of Hg
   4) All have same weight

24. The mass of 1 mole of electrons is
   1) 9.1×10^{-28} g
   2) 1.008 mg
   3) 0.55 mg
   4) 9.1×10^{-27} g

25. The maximum number of molecules are present in
   1) 15 L of H_2 gas at STP
   2) 5 L of N_2 gas at STP
   3) 0.5 g of H_2 gas
   4) 10 g of O_2 gas

26. Which of the following contains greatest number of oxygen atoms?
   1) 1 g of O
   2) 1 g of O_2
   3) 1 g of O_3
   4) All have the same number of atoms

27. The numerical value of $\frac{N}{n}$ (where, N is the number of molecules in a given sample of gas and n is the number of moles of the gas) is
   1) 8.314
   2) 6.02×10^{23}
   3) 0.0821
   4) 1.66×10^{-19}
   5) 1.62×10^{-24}

28. Number of atoms of oxygen present in 10.6 g of Na_2CO_3 will be
   1) 6.02×10^{23}
   2) 12.04×10^{22}
   3) 1.806×10^{23}
   4) 31.80×10^{28}

29. 4.6×10^{22} atoms of an element weigh 13.8 g. The atomic weight of element is

   1) 290
   2) 180
   3) 34.4
   4) 10.4

30. One gram mole of a gas at NTP occupies 22.4 L. This fact was derived from
   1) Law of gaseous volumes
   2) Avogadro's hypothesis
   3) Berzelius hypothesis
   4) Dalton's atomic theory

31. Weight of an atom of an element is 6.644×10^{-23} g. What will be the number of g atom of that element in 40 kg?
   1) 10^3
   2) 10^6
   3) 1.5×10^3
   4) None of these

32. Arrange the following in the order of increasing mass (atomic mass; O = 16, Cu = 63, N = 14)
   1. One atom of oxygen
   2. One atom of nitrogen
   3. 1×10^{-10} mole of oxygen
   4. 1×10^{-10} mole of copper

   1) $II < I < III < IV$
   2) $I < II < III < IV$
   3) $III < II < IV < I$
   4) $IV < II < III < I$
   5) $II < IV < I < III$

33. How many moles of magnesium phosphate, $Mg_3(PO_4)_2$ will contain 0.25 mole of oxygen atoms?
   1) 0.02
   2) 3.125×10^{-2}
   3) 1.25×10^{-2}
   4) 2.5×10^{-2}

34. The total number of protons in 10 g of calcium carbonate is $(N_0 = 6.023 \times 10^{23})$

   1) 3.01×10^{24}
   2) 4.06×10^{24}
   3) 2.01×10^{24}
   4) 3.02×10^{24}

35. The number of molecules of CO_2 present in 44 g of CO_2 is
   1) 6.0×10^{23}
   2) 3×10^{23}
   3) 12×10^{23}
   4) 3×10^{10}

36. Which of the following has the smallest number of molecules?
   1) 0.1 mole of CO_2 gas
   2) 11.2 L of CO_2 gas at STP
   3) 22 g of CO_2 gas
   4) 22.4×10^3 mL of CO_2 gas at STP

37. 2 g of O_2 at 0^0C and 760 mm of Hg pressure has volume
   1) 1.4 L
   2) 2.8 L
   3) 11.2 L
   4) 22.4 L

38. Which one of the following has maximum number of atoms of oxygen?
   1) 2 g of carbon monoxide
   2) 2 g of carbon dioxide
   3) 2 g of sulphur dioxide
   4) 2 g of water

39. Number of atoms of He in 100 u of He (atomic weight of He is 4) are

   1) 25
   2) 100
   3) 50
   4) $100 \times 6 \times 10^{-23}$

40. Which of the following is correct for
   C(graphite) + O_2 (gas) $\rightarrow$ CO_2 , heat $= -348$ kJ?
   1) Heat absorbed
   2) Mass of product > Mass of reactant
   3) Mass of product < Mass of reactant
   4) Mass of product = Mass of reactant

41. A signature, written in carbon pencil weights 1 mg. What is the number of carbon atoms present in the signature?
   1) 5.02×10^{23}
   2) 5.02×10^{20}
   3) 6.02×10^{20}
   4) 0.502×10^{20}

42. Which of the following contains maximum number of molecules?
   1) 100 cc of CO_2 at STP
   2) 150 cc of N_2 at STP
   3) 50 cc of SO_2 at STP
   4) 150 cc of O_2 at STP
   5) 200 cc of NH_3 at STP

43. The mass of $112 cm^3$ of CH_4 gas at STP is
   1) 0.16 g
   2) 0.8 g
   3) 0.08 g
   4) 1.6 g

44. Number of atoms in 560 g of Fe (atomic mass 56 g mol^{-1}) is
   1) Twice that of 70 g N
   2) Half that of 20 g H
   3) Both are correct
   4) None of these

45. Mass of 0.1 mole of methane is
   1) 1 g
   2) 16 g
   3) 1.6 g
   4) 0.1 g

46. 74.5 g of a metallic chloride contains 35.5 g of chlorine, the equivalent weight of the metal is
   1) 19.5
   2) 35.5
   3) 39
   4) 78.0

47. 2 g of metal carbonate is neutralised completely by 100 mL of 0.1 (N) HCl. The equivalent weight of metal carbonate is
   1) 50
   2) 100
   3) 150
   4) 200

48. $KMnO_4$ (mol.wt.= 158) oxidizes oxalic acid in acid medium to CO_2 and water as follows
   $$5C_2O_4^{2-} + 2MnO_4^- + 16H^+ \rightarrow 10CO_2 + 2Mn^{2+} + 8H_2O$$
   What is the equivalent weight of $KMnO_4$?
   1) 158
   2) 31.6
   3) 39.5
   4) 79

49. 3 g of an oxide of a metal is converted to chloride completely and it yielded 5 g of chloride. The equivalent weight of the metal is
   1) 33.25
   2) 3.325
   3) 12
   4) 20

50. The formula mass of Mohr's salt is 392. The iron present in it is oxidised by $KMnO_4$ in acid medium. The equivalent mass of Mohr's salt is
   1) 392
   2) 31.6
   3) 278
   4) 156

Single Correct Answer Type

1 **(3)**

$$\text{Average value} = \frac{25.2 + 25.25 + 25.0}{1} = \frac{75.45}{3}$$

$= 25.15 = 25.2 \text{ mL}$

Number of significant figure is 3.

2 **(2)**

$4.523 + 2.3 + 6.24 = 13.063$. As 2.3 has least number of decimal places $i.\,e.$, one, therefore sum should be reported to one decimal place only. After rounding off, reported sum=13.1 which has three significant figures.

3 **(2)**

As, we know that least count of the instrument is equal to the most possible error of the instrument hence, least count of the instrument will be 0.01 cm.

4 **(5)**

Smallest and largest amount of energy respectively eV and L-atm.

$1 \text{ eV} = 1.6 \times 10^{-19} \text{J}$

$1 \text{ L} - \text{atm} = 101.325 \text{ J}$

5 **(4)**

The amu represents atomic mass unit. It is used in place of unified mass unit.

$1 \text{ u} = 1 \text{ Avogram} = 1 \text{ Aston} = 1 \text{ Dalton}$

$1 \text{ u} = \dfrac{1}{12} \times \text{mass of C} - 12 \text{ atom}$

$= \dfrac{1}{12} \times 1.9924 \times 10^{-23} \text{g}$

$\qquad\qquad = 1.66 \times 10^{-24} \text{g} = 1.66 \times 10^{-27} \text{ kg}$

6 **(1)**

$22.4 \text{ L} = 17 \text{ g}$

$11.2 \text{ L} = \dfrac{17}{22.4} \times 11.2 = 8.5\text{g}$

7 **(5)**

N_2O and NO verify the law of multiple proportions.

8 **(2)**

$$\text{Mole of sucrose} = \frac{\text{mass of sucrose (in gram)}}{\text{molecular weight of sucrose}}$$

$$= \frac{25.6}{342.3} = 0.0747882$$

Formula of sucrose $= C_{12}H_{22}O_{11}$

Number of H atoms in 1 mole of sucrose

$= 22 \times 6.023 \times 10^{23}$

Number of H atoms in 0.0747882 mole of sucrose

$= 22 \times 6.023 \times 10^{23} \times 0.074788 = 9.9 \times 10^{23}$

9   **(4)**

Number of moles of oxygen $= \dfrac{80}{16}$

Number of atoms of oxygen $= \dfrac{80}{16} \times N_0 \times 2$

$$= 5 \times N_0 \times 2$$

Number of moles in 5 g of hydrogen $= \dfrac{5}{1}$

Number of atoms in 5 g of hydrogen $= 5 \times N_0 \times 2$

Hence, the number of atoms in 80 g of oxygen is equal to the number of atoms in5 g of hydrogen.

10   **(2)**

Gram molecular volume of oxygen at STP is 5.6L or 5600 cm^3.

11   **(4)**

Mol. wt. of C_2H_5OH

$= 12 \times 2 + 1 \times 5 + 16 + 1 = 46$ g

$\because$ 46 g of C_2H_5OH has hydrogen atoms

$= 6 \times$ Avogadro number

$\therefore$ 0.046 g of C_2H_5OH has hydrogen atoms

$$= \dfrac{6 \times 6.023 \times 10^{23} \times 0.046}{46}$$

$= 3.6 \times 10^{21}$ atoms of hydrogen.

12   **(3)**

5.   Atoms in 2.0 molof

$$S_8 = 2 \times 8 \times 6.02 \times 10^{23}$$

$$= 9.632 \times 10^{24}$$

2. Atoms in 6.0 mol of $S = 6 \times 6.02 \times 10^{23}$

$$= 3.612 \times 10^{24}$$

6.   Atoms in 5.5 mol of

$SO_2 = 3 \times 5.5 \times 6.02 \times 10^{23} = 9.93 \times 10^{24}$

7.   Atoms in 4.48 L of CO_2 at STP $= \dfrac{3 \times 4.48 \times 6.02 \times 10^{23}}{22.4}$

$$= 3.612 \times 10^{23}$$

13   **(1)**

Given vapour density $= 11.2$

Molecular weight $= 2 \times 11.2 = 22.4$

$\therefore 22.4$ g of gas occupies $= 22.4$ L at STP

$\therefore 1$ g of gas occupies $= \dfrac{22.4}{22.4} \times 1 = 1$ L at STP

14   **(1)**

Weight of $NH_3 = 4.25g$

We know that number of atoms in 1 mole or 17 g of

$NH_3 = 4 \times 6.023 \times 10^{23}$

$\therefore$ Number of atom in 4.25 g of

$$NH_3 = \frac{4 \times 6.023 \times 10^{23}}{17} \times 4.25$$

$$= 6.023 \times 10^{23}$$

15   **(1)**

$$\because 0.1 \text{mole of carbohydrate contains} = 1 \text{ g of hydrogen.}$$

$$\therefore 1 \text{ mole of carbohydrate contains} = \frac{1}{0.1}$$

$= 10$ g hydrogen

Hence, its molecular formula $= C_5H_{10}O_5$.

16   **(4)**

The law of constant composition—According to this law, "A chemical compound is always found to be made up of the same elements combined together in the same proportions by weights".

This law is same as law of definite proportions.

17   **(4)**

One mole of CO_2 contains 6.02×10^{23} atoms of carbon and 6.023×10^{23} molecules of oxygen.

18   **(2)**

Number of gram molecules $= \dfrac{6.02 \times 10^{25}}{6.02 \times 10^{23}} = 100$

19   **(1)**

Number of atoms in 24 g of $C = \frac{24}{12} \times 6.02 \times 10^{23}$

$= 2 \times 6.02 \times 10^{23}$

Number of atoms in

56 g of $Fe = \frac{56}{56} \times 6.02 \times 10^{23}$

Number of atoms in

26 g of $Al = \frac{26}{27} \times 6.02 \times 10^{23}$

$$\approx 6.02 \times 10^{23}$$

Number of atoms in 108 g of $Ag = \frac{108}{108} \times 6.02 \times 10^{23}$

$= 6.02 \times 10^{23}$

20   **(1)**

$CaF_2 = 146.4$ g

Molecular weight of $CaF_2 = 78.08$ g/mol

$$\text{Moles of } CaF_2 = \frac{\text{weight}}{\text{molecular weight}}$$

$$= \frac{146.4}{78.08} = 1.875 \text{ mol}$$

Number of formula units of

CaF_2 in 146.4 g of CaF_2

$$= \text{No. of moles} \times 6.022 \times 10^{23}$$

$$= 1.875 \times 6.022 \times 10^{23}$$

$$= 11.29 \times 10^{23}$$

$$= 1.129 \times 10^{24} CaF_2$$

21   **(4)**

$$\text{Moles} = \frac{\text{mass}}{\text{molecular mass}}$$

Given,   mass of $Al_2(SO_4)_3 = 50$g

Molecular mass of $Al_2(SO_4)_3 = 342$ g

$\therefore$ Moles of $Al_2(SO_4)_3 = \frac{50}{342} = 0.14$ mol

22   **(1)**

Given, volume of $O_2 = 1$L

$$\because 22.4 \text{ L of } O_2 \text{ at STP} = 32 \text{ g}$$

$$\therefore 1 \text{ L of } O_2 \text{ at STP} = \frac{32}{22.4} \text{ g}$$

$$= 1.43 \text{ g}$$

23   **(1)**

(a) Density of water $= 1$ g cm^{-3}

Mass of water $= 1$ m$^3 = 10^6$ cm^{-3}

Mass $=$ volume $\times$ density

$= 10^6$ cm$^{-3} \times 1$ g cm^{-3}

$= 10^6$

$= \frac{10^6}{10^3}$ kg

$= 1000$ kg

(b) Mass of normal adult man $= 65$ kg

(c) Density of Hg $= 13.6$ g cm^{-3}

Volume of Hg $= 10$L $= 10 \times 1000$ cm^{-3}

$$\therefore \text{Mass of Hg} = 13.6 \times 10 \times 1000$$

$= 136000\,g$

$= 13.6\,kg$

$\therefore$ Mass of $1m^3$ water is highest.

24   **(3)**

One mole of electrons$= 6.023 \times 10^{23}$ electrons

Mass of one electron$=9.1 \times 10^{-28}g$

Mass of one mole of electrons

$= 6.023 \times 10^{23} \times 9.1 \times 10^{-28}g$

$= 5.48 \times 10^{-4}g= 0.548\,mg$

$\approx 0.55\,mg$

25   **(1)**

In 15 L of H_2 gas at STP, the number of molecules

$$= \frac{6.023 \times 10^{23}}{22.4} \times 15$$

$$= 4.033 \times 10^{23}$$

In 5 L of N_2 gas at STP, the number of molecules

$$= \frac{6.023 \times 10^{23} \times 5}{22.4} = 1.344 \times 10^{23}$$

In 0.5 g of H_2 gas, the number of molecules

$$= \frac{6.023 \times 10^{23} \times 0.5}{2}$$

$$= 1.505 \times 10^{23}$$

In 10 g of O_2 gas, the number of molecules

$$= \frac{6.023 \times 10^{23} \times 10}{32}$$

$$= 1.882 \times 10^{23}$$

Hence, maximum molecules are present in 15L of H_2 at STP.

26   **(4)**

Number of atoms $=$ moles $\times N_A \times$ atomicity

Here, $N_A=$ Avogadro's number

(a) Number of oxygen atoms in 1 g of O

$$= \frac{1}{16} \times N_A \times 1$$

$$= \frac{N_A}{16}$$

(b)Number of oxygen atoms in 1 g of O_2

$$= \frac{1}{32} \times N_A \times 2$$

$$= \frac{N_A}{16}$$

(c) Number of oxygen atoms in 1 g of O_3

$$= \frac{1}{48} N_A \times 3 = \frac{N_A}{16}$$

Hence, all have the same number of oxygen atoms.

27   **(2)**

Number of molecules in n moles of substance$= n \times N_0$

$$= n \times 6.023 \times 10^{23}$$

$$\frac{N \text{ (no. of molecules)}}{n \text{ (no. of moles)}} = ?$$

$$= \frac{n \times 6.023 \times 10^{23}}{n} = 6.023 \times 10^{23}$$

28   **(3)**

Molecular mass of Na_2CO_3

$$= 2 \times 23 + 12 + 3 \times 16 = 106$$

$\therefore$ 106 g Na_2CO_3 contains

$$= 3 \times 6.023 \times 10^{23} \text{ oxygen atoms}$$

$\therefore$ 10.6 g of Na_2CO_3 will contain

$$= \frac{3 \times 6.023 \times 10^{23}}{106} \times 10.6$$

$$= 18.069 \times 10^{22}$$

$$= 1.806 \times 10^{23} \text{ oxygen atoms}$$

29   **(2)**

4.6×10^{22} atoms weight $= 13.8$ g

Hence, 6.02×10^{23} atoms will weigh

$$= \frac{13.8 \times 6.02 \times 10^{23}}{4.6 \times 10^{22}} = 108.6 \text{ g (molar mass)}$$

30   **(2)**

According to Avogadro's hypothesis one gram mole of a gas at NTP occupies 22.4 L.

31   **(1)**

Number of atoms in 40 kg$= \dfrac{40 \times 10^3 \text{g}}{6.644 \times 10^{-23} \text{ g}}$

($\because$ Weight of an atom$= 6.644 \times 10^{-23}$ g)

$$= 6.02 \times 10^{26}$$

$\therefore$ Number of gram atoms of element in 40 kg

$$= \frac{6.02 \times 10^{26}}{6.02 \times 10^{23}} = 10^3$$

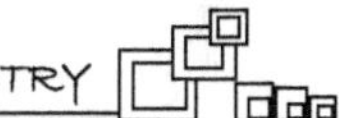

32 **(1)**

1. Mass of one atom of oxygen =

$$\frac{16}{6.022 \times 10^{23}} = 2.66 \times 10^{-23}\text{g}$$

2. Mass of one atom of nitrogen

$$= \frac{14}{6.022 \times 10^{23}} = 2.32 \times 10^{-23}\text{g}$$

3. Mass of 1×10^{-10} mole of oxygen

$$= 16 \times 10^{-10}\text{g}$$

4. Mass of 1×10^{-10} mole of copper

$$= 63 \times 10^{-10}$$

Hence, masses of atoms in increasing order

$$\text{II} < \text{I} < \text{III} < \text{IV}$$

33 **(2)**

$$Mg_3(PO_4)_2; \text{mole}$$

8 mole of O-atom are contained by 1 mole $Mg_3(PO_4)_2$.

Hence, 0.25 moles of O-atom $= \frac{1}{8} \times 0.25$ mole $Mg_3(PO_4)_2$

$$= 3.125 \times 10^{-2}$$

34 **(1)**

We know that protons in 1 mole $CaCO_3$

=atomic number of calcium + atomic number of carbon + 3 (atomic number of oxygen)

$$= 20 + 6 + 3(8) = 50 \text{ mol}$$

$\therefore$ Proton in 10 g $CaCO_3 = \dfrac{10 \times 50}{100} \times 6.02 \times 10^{23}$

$$= 3.01 \times 10^{24}$$

35 **(1)**

1 mole=molecular mass in gram=6.02×10^{23} molecules

Given mass of $CO_2 = 44$ g

Molecular mass of $CO_2 = 12 + 16 \times 2 = 44$

$\therefore$ No. of molecules in 44 g of $CO_2 = 6.02 \times 10^{23}$

36 **(1)**

(a) 0.1 mole of CO_2

(b) $\frac{11.2}{22.4} = 0.5$ mole of CO_2

(c) $\frac{22}{44} = 0.5$ mole of CO_2

(d) $\frac{22.4 \times 10^3}{22400} = 1$ mole of CO_2

Equal numbers of moles have equal number of molecules.

Hence, the smallest number of molecules of CO_2 is in 0.1 mole of CO_2.

37 **(1)**

Given mass of O_2 = 2 g at 0°C and 760 mm Hg

32 g of O_2 = 22.4 L at STP

$\therefore \qquad$ 2 g of $O_2 = \dfrac{22.4}{32} \times 2 = 1.4$ L

38 **(4)**

Number of oxygen atom in 2 g of CO

$$= \dfrac{2}{28} \times 6.022 \times 10^{23} \times 1$$

Number of oxygen atom in 2 g of CO_2

$$= \dfrac{2}{44} \times 6.022 \times 10^{23} \times 2$$

Number of oxygen atom in 2 g of SO_2

$$= \dfrac{2}{64} \times 6.022 \times 10^{23} \times 2$$

Number of oxygen atom in 2 g of H_2O

$$= \dfrac{2}{18} \times 6.022 \times 10^{23} \times 1$$

Hence, 2 g of H_2O has maximum number of atoms of oxygen.

39 **(1)**

$$\because 4\,u = 1\text{ He atom}$$

$$\therefore 1\,u = \dfrac{1}{4}\text{ He atom}$$

Hence, $100\,u = \dfrac{1 \times 100}{4} = 25$ atoms

40 **(4)**

$C_{graphite} + O_2(g) \rightarrow CO_2; \Delta H = -348$ kJ

12 g $\qquad$ 32 g $\qquad$ 44 g

In the above reaction, heat is evolved and mass of product is equal to mass of reactant.

41 **(4)**

$\because$ Number of atoms present in 12 g carbon

$= 6.023 \times 10^{23}$

$\therefore$ No. of atoms present in 1 mg carbon

$$= \dfrac{6.023 \times 10^{23} \times 1}{12 \times 1000}$$

$= 0.502 \times 10^{20}$

42 **(5)**

200 cc of NH_3 at STP contains maximum number of molecules because NH_3 compound has

lowest molecular weight and highest volume than other compounds.

43   (3)

$$\because \text{Mass of } 22400 \text{ cm}^3 \text{ of } CH_4 \text{ at STP} = 16 \text{ g}$$

$$\therefore \quad \text{Mass of } 1 \text{ cm}^3 \text{ of } CH_4 \text{ at STP} = \frac{16}{22400} \text{ g}$$

$$\therefore \text{Mass of } 112 \text{ cm}^3 \text{ of } CH_4 \text{ at STP} = \frac{16}{22400} \times 112$$

$$= 0.08 \text{ g}$$

44   (3)

Moles of Fe $= \dfrac{560}{56} = 10$

Moles of N $= \dfrac{70}{14} = 5$

Moles of H $= \dfrac{20}{1} = 20$

Equal number of moles have equal number of atoms.

Hence, number of atoms in 560 g of Fe is twice that of 70 g N and is half that of 20 g of H.

45   (3)

Mass of 1 mole of methane $(CH_4) = 16$ g

Mass of 0.1 mole of methane $= 16 \times 0.1$ g $= 1.6$ g

46   (3)

Equivalent weight of metal

$$= \frac{\text{wt. of metal}}{\text{wt. of chlorine}} \times 35.5$$

$$= \frac{(74.5 - 35.5) \times 35.5}{35.5} = 39$$

47   (4)

Number of gram equivalents of

$$HCl = \frac{100 \times 0.1}{1000} = 0.01$$

Number of gram equivalents of HCl=Number of gram equivalents of metal carbonate

$$0.01 = 0.01$$

Therefore, mass of 1 g equivalents of carbonate salt

$$= \frac{2}{0.01} = 200 \text{g}$$

Equivalent mass of metal carbonate=200

48   (2)

$$5C_2O_4^{2-} + \overset{+7}{2MnO_4^-} + 16H^+ \rightarrow 10CO_2 + 2Mn^{2+} + 8H_2O$$

$$\text{Equivalent weight} = \frac{\text{molecular weight}}{\text{change in oxidation number}} = \frac{158}{5} = 31.6$$

49   **(1)**

$$\frac{\text{Wt. of metal oxide}}{\text{Wt. of metal chloride}}$$

$$= \frac{\text{Eq. wt. of metal} + \text{Eq. wt. of oxide}}{\text{Eq. wt. of metal} + \text{Eq. wt. of chloride}}$$

$$\frac{3}{5} = \frac{E + 8}{E + 35.5}$$

$$E = 33.25$$

50   **(1)**

Mohr's salt is $(NH_4)_2SO_4 . FeSO_4 . 6H_2O$

The equation is

$$5Fe^{2+} + MnO_4^- + 8H^+ \rightarrow 5Fe^{3+} + Mn^{2+} + 4H_2O$$

Total change in oxidation number of iron

$$= (+3) - (+2)$$

$$= +1$$

So, equivalent wt. of Mohr's salt

$$= \frac{\text{Mol. wt. of Mohr's salt}}{1}$$

$$= \frac{392}{1}$$

$$= 392$$

www.ingramcontent.com/pod-product-compliance
Lightning Source LLC
Chambersburg PA
CBHW051939150726
47999CB00006B/2295